The Little Book of PLANTS

By Zack Bush and Laurie Friedman
Illustrated by Vitor Lopes

THIS BOOK BELONGS TO:

MARTY TO A.K.A Little Guy.

Copyright © 2023 Publishing Power, LLC
All Rights Reserved
All inquiries about this book can be sent
to the author at info@thelittlebookof.com
Published in the United States by Publishing Power, LLC
ISBN: 978-1-959141-27-3
For more information, visit our website:
www.BooksByZackAndLaurie.com
Paperback

PLANTS.
They're all around you.
But what are they exactly?
And why are they important?

There's so much to know about **PLANTS.**
Ready to learn? Just turn the page!

A **PLANT** is a living thing that grows on the earth.

PLANTS come in all shapes and sizes.
There are . . .

BIG TREES.

MEDIUM-SIZED BUSHES.

SMALL FLOWERS.

AND TINY FERNS, HERBS, AND MOSSES.

Scientists who study **PLANTS** are called botanists.

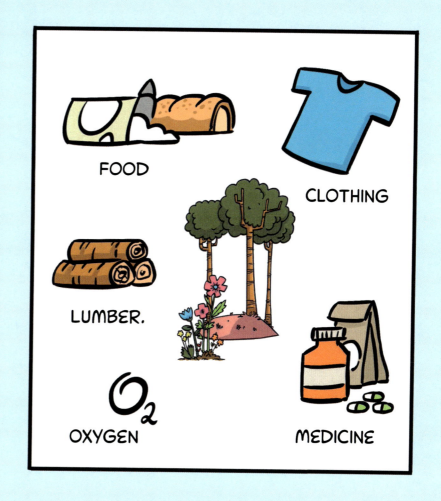

Botany is important because people and animals depend on **PLANTS** for so many things.

Through a process called photosynthesis, **PLANTS** produce oxygen that all people and animals need to breathe and survive.

Here's how it works: **PLANTS** convert light from the sun into food. **PLANTS** use the food to grow. As **PLANTS** grow, they produce oxygen. People and animals breathe in the oxygen made by **PLANTS.**

PLANTS that people use for food are grown on farms. These **CROPS** include fruits and vegetables and even rice and beans.

Farmers work hard taking care of their **CROPS**.

Once the **CROPS** are grown, they're picked, boxed, and shipped to grocery stores . . .

And to markets where people buy the food they need to live.

There are so many delicious foods that come from **PLANTS.** Which are your favorites?

In addition to food, many farmers grow **CROPS** that are used for the clothing we wear.

Crops such as cotton are taken to factories to make items like jeans and T-shirts.

Other farmers grow trees that provide the lumber needed to build houses and buildings.

Some farmers even grow **PLANTS** that are used as medicines.

Humans aren't the only beings who depend on **PLANTS**. Animals do too. Animals in the wild need **PLANTS** not only for food but also for shelter.

If you look at a **PLANT**, you will see that most have three basic parts:
Roots.
Stems.
And leaves.

The roots of a **PLANT** grow underground. Roots help to keep the **PLANT** from falling over. Roots also gather water and minerals from the soil that feed the **PLANT** and help it grow.

The stem is the part of the **PLANT** that supports leaves and flowers. Stems also help move food and water around the **PLANT.**

The leaves of a **PLANT** also play an important role. The job of the leaves is to capture sunlight and convert it into energy for growth.

Leaves come in lots of shapes and sizes.

In addition to all of the things **PLANTS** provide, they also make the world a more beautiful place.

When you go to the park, take a moment to look at all of the **PLANTS** around you.
What do you see?

Big **PLANTS**.
Little **PLANTS**.
Colorful **PLANTS**.

There are lots of ways that you can enjoy and have fun with **PLANTS!** You can visit a nursery where plants are grown.

You can paint or draw different kinds of PLANTS.

You can learn to garden and grow **PLANTS** yourself.

You can even make special gifts from **PLANTS** to give to others.

CONGRATULATIONS!
Now you know so much about **PLANTS.**

Here's your **PLANTS** badge.
Go ahead. Print it out, pin it on, and start having fun with **PLANTS** today.

Go to the website www.BooksByZackAndLaurie.com and print out your badges from the Printables & Activities page.

And if you like this book, please go to Amazon and leave a kind review.

Keep reading all of the books in #thelittlebookof series to learn new things and earn more badges. Other books in the series include:

VALUES/EMOTIONS

The Little Book of Kindness
The Little Book of Patience
The Little Book of Confidence
The Little Book of Positivity
The Little Book of Love
The Little Book of Good Deeds
The Little Book of Responsibility
The Little Book of Curiosity
The Little Book of Gratitude
The Little Book of Friendship
The Little Book of Laughter
The Little Book of Creativity
The Little Book of Honesty
The Little Book of Imagination
The Little Book of Happiness
The Little Book of Sharing
The Little Book of Listening
The Little Book of Hope

ACTIVITIES/IDEAS

The Little Book of Camping
The Little Book of Sports
The Little Book of Music
The Little Book of Government
The Little Book of the Supreme Court
The Little Book of Transportation
The Little Book of Presidential Elections
The Little Book of Grandparents
The Little Book of Bedtime
The Little Book of Good Manners
The Little Book of Dance
The Little Book of Yoga
The Little Book of Healthy Habits
The Little Book of Setting Goals
The Little Book of Organization
The Little Book of Teamwork
The Little Book of Baking
The Little Book of Cooking
The Little Book of Mindfulness

SCIENCE/NATURE

The Little Book of Nature
The Little Book of Outer Space
The Little Book of Going Green
The Little Book of Weather
The Little Book of Pets
The Little Book of Dinosaurs

MILESTONES/HOLIDAYS

The Little Book of Kindergarten
The Little Book of First Grade
The Little Book of Valentine's Day
The Little Book of Father's Day
The Little Book of Halloween
The Little Book of Giving (Holiday Edition)
The Little Book of Santa Claus
The Little Book of Going Back to School

Made in the USA
Middletown, DE
06 January 2024

47329963R00024